C000002311

MEMORIES OF
CHESTERFIELD

TRUE NORTH BOOKS

DEAN CLOUGH
HALIFAX
WEST YORKSHIRE
HX3 5AX
TEL 01422 344344

THE PUBLISHERS WOULD LIKE TO THANK THE
FOLLOWING COMPANIES FOR SUPPORTING THE
PRODUCTION OF THIS BOOK

WD BOTHAM & SONS

BRAMPTON BAKERY

COALITE GROUP LIMITED

CROWDER & ALDERSON FUNERAL SERVICES

EYRES OF CHESTERFIELD

FREDERICKS ICE CREAM

GK NORTHERN LIMITED

MANOR COLLEGE

MOUNT ST. MARY'S COLLEGE

First published in Great Britain by True North Books
Dean Clough
Halifax HX3 5AX
1998

All rights reserved. No part of this publication may be reproduced, stored in a
retrieval system, or transmitted in any form, or by any means, electronic, mechanical,
photocopy, recording or otherwise without the prior permission in writing of the
Copyright holders, nor be otherwise circulated in any form or binding or cover other
than in which it is published and without a similar condition being imposed on the
subsequent publisher.

© TRUE NORTH HOLDINGS
ISBN 1 900 463 61 X

Introduction

Knifesmithgate, looking east to Stephenson Place around 1955.

Welcome to *Memories of Chesterfield,* a look back on some of the places, events and people in the town which have shaped our lives over a period of around half a century. The following pages are brought to life by the selection of images from the not-too-distant past, chosen according to their ability to rekindle memories of days gone by and show how people used to shop, work and play in the town where they grew up. Modern image reproduction techniques have enabled us to present these pictures in a way rarely seen before, and the lively design and informative text has attempted to set the book apart from some of the other works available. The chosen period covered here is one which contains events within the memory of a large number of people in Chesterfield - this is not a book about crinolines or bowler-hats! Neither is *Memories of Chesterfield* a work of local history in the normal sense of the term. It has far more to do with entertainment than serious study, but we hope you will agree it is none the worse for that. We hope that the following pages will prompt readers' own memories of Chesterfield from days gone by - and we are always delighted to hear from people who can add to the information contained in the captions so that we can enhance future reprints of the book. Many local companies and organisations have allowed us to study their archives and include their history - and fascinating reading it makes too. The present-day guardians of the companies concerned are proud of their products, the achievements of their people and the hard work of their forefathers whose efforts created these long established firms in the first place. We are pleased to play our part by making it possible for them to share their history with a wider audience.

When we began compiling *Memories of Chesterfield* several months ago we anticipated that the task would be a pleasurable one, but our expectations were greatly surpassed. The quality of the photographs we have been privileged to use has been superb, and the assistance we have received from Mr. G. W. Martin, an enthusiast for everything concerned with the history of his town, not forgetting staff at Chesterfield's Reference Library, made our work very enjoyable. Mr. Martin deserves our very special thanks, for many of the photographs included here were taken by him, and much of the text was compiled from information he supplied. It was a tremendous pleasure working with him on the book.

There is a growing appetite for all things 'nostalgic' and we are pleased to have played a small part in swelling the number of images and associated information available to the growing number of enthusiasts. There is much talk in modern times about the regeneration of the local economy, the influx of new industries and the challenge of attracting new enterprise from other regions to the town. And quite right too. We could, however, make the mistake of thinking that the changes are all happening *now,* but the reality is that there have always been major developments going on in the area. 'Change' is relentless and the photographs on the pages of the book serve to remind us of a mere selection of them. Some of the images fall outside the qualification we describe as 'within living memory', but most of these will be familiar to us, either because they concern an event described to us by a close relative, or they feature monuments such as the businesses or buildings we simply felt compelled to mention. Whatever the view taken on the boundaries which separate 'history', 'nostalgia' and the present time, we should all invest a few moments occasionally to reflect on the past and the events which made our town what it is today.

Memories of Chesterfield has been a pleasure to compile, we sincerely hope you enjoy reading it.

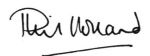

Happy memories!
Phil Holland

PHOTOGRAPHS COMPILED BY MARK SMITH
CAPTIONS COMPILED BY PHIL HOLLAND
DESIGN BY MANDY WALKER
LOCAL BUSINESS CONTENT BY ANDREW HALES

Contents

Right: The coronation of Her Majesty Queen Elizabeth II in June 1953 was a welcome cause of rejoicing throughout Britain. The royal couple were tremendously popular and the coronation provided a rare excuse for a national celebration in the difficult first decade after the end of the Second War. Street parties, the decoration of shops and public buildings and a general air of anticipation and excitement filled the town. This delightful photograph features a Chesterfield Transport double-decker - made by Crossleys - waiting at its pick-up point on Rose Hill. Records show that the vehicle was built in 1947, and was one of 30 similar buses to be acquired by the Corporation. It was sold in 1966. Behind the bus is the Town Hall, unusually up-staged by the tremendous effort which went into decorating the vehicle. Keen eyes may just be able to make out the grassed areas to the right and left of the double-decker. These are now covered in tarmac and serve as large car parks.

Events and occasions

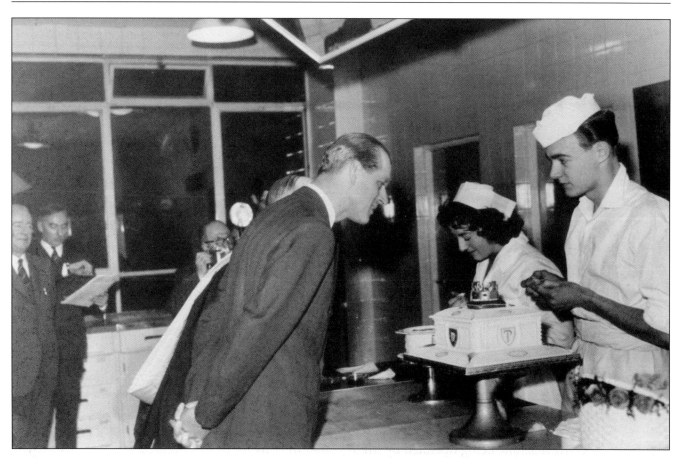

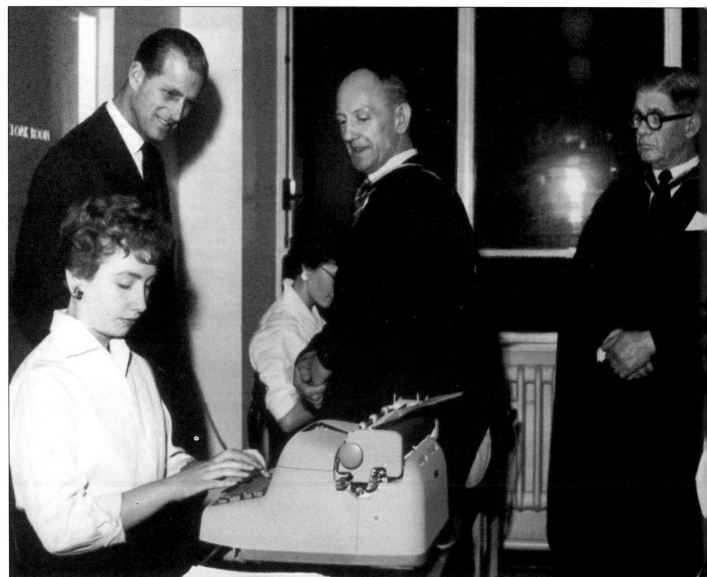

Left: Part of the 1958 visit saw the Duke of Edinburgh tour the College Bakery Department. This picture shows him studying a cake which had obviously been prepared for this visit - the clues being the prominent "P" and the royal crest on top of it. A photographer can be seen recording the scene from the other side of the action - perhaps the snap found its way into that week's local paper? Notice the upright gent in the background. He looks at his watch and studies his clip-board, doing his best to keep the Prince on schedule throughout the tour.

Below left: When Prince Philip visited Chesterfield in 1958 called at the "Advanced Typing Pool" of the college, taking a particular interest in the nimble fingers and electric machine being operated by Miss June Alton. Also present was College Principal Mr E. Cardwell (centre) and his stern-looking colleague.

Below: An historic scene captured along Hope Street in Brampton. The gathering was organised in order to celebrate the Silver Jubilee of King George V and Queen Mary, and was typical of many which took place in Chesterfield and beyond. It would have taken considerable skill and determination to organise a spread like this with the very limited resources available to ladies in the 1930s.

No doubt the children would have appreciated the event, and remembered it for many years to come. Many of the children seen here will be in their seventies at the time of writing and their parents, if they survive, in their nineties.

Sadly we know few of the names of the people in the picture, but we know that the tiny tot in the foreground was Baby Beryl Platts.

> "THE JUBILEE OF KING GEORGE V IN 1935 WAS CELEBRATED IN GREAT STYLE"

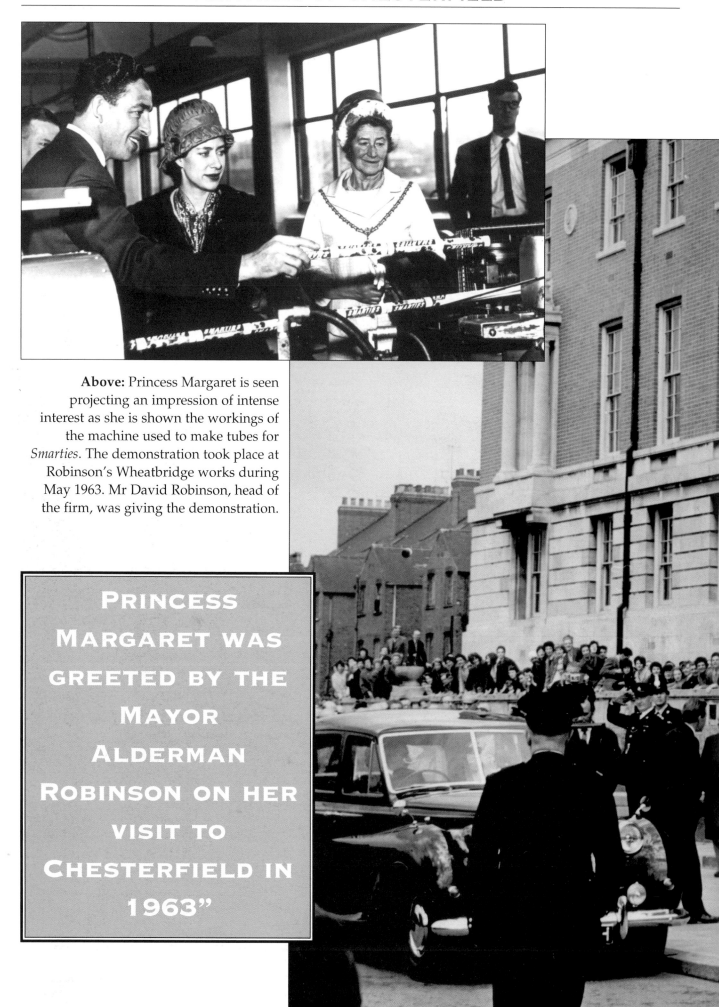

Above: Princess Margaret is seen projecting an impression of intense interest as she is shown the workings of the machine used to make tubes for *Smarties*. The demonstration took place at Robinson's Wheatbridge works during May 1963. Mr David Robinson, head of the firm, was giving the demonstration.

PRINCESS MARGARET WAS GREETED BY THE MAYOR ALDERMAN ROBINSON ON HER VISIT TO CHESTERFIELD IN 1963"

Below: Loyal subjects gather outside the Town Hall for the visit of the Princess Margaret to Chesterfield. The photograph dates from 1963. The Princess is seen here walking towards the Mayor Alderman Robinson and the Mayoress waiting on the steps of the Town Hall to greet her. While in Chesterfield the Princess visited a number of leading companies, including Robinsons.

Left: This photograph was taken to commemorate the visit of the Cardiff Salvation Army Band to Chesterfield in 1956. They caused quite a stir in the town when they paraded around it, playing as they went. The picture was taken on the Town Hall steps and shows members of the band with the Mayor, Alderman William Weston.

Above: The visit of Cardiff Salvation Army Band resulted in several pictures being taken as they marched through the town centre behind their brass band. This picture shows them marching through West Bars on their way to the town centre. Just above the heads of the marchers a wall clock can be seen jutting out from the building there. All the properties from this clock right up to the shop on the right hand edge of this scene have since been pulled down and replaced with modern retail shops.

Above: Whit Walks have been a feature of religious life in Chesterfield for many years. More often than not they would be the subject of several commemorative photographs, and this one, in 1963 was no exception. In modern times the walk takes place on Spring Bank Holiday Monday, whereas at one time it would be Whit Monday. This was the case back in 1963 when this picture was taken. The religious parade would include members of the Methodist, Baptist, and Unitarian churches, along with decorated floats and carts, marching bands and youth organisations. This photograph shows part of the route, along Tennyson Avenue, returning to the Market Place and being led by the Mayor (centre), Alderman Ernest Bradbury Robinson, on his right was the Right Reverend Douglas Wollen (the Mayor's Chaplain) and the Rev. T. A.Taylor of the Baptist Church. The group was followed by the Salvation Army Band.

Below: One of the floats in the 1963 Whitsuntide Walk, no doubt hoping to win one of the prizes in the judging ceremony which was about to follow. Along the side of the horse drawn vehicle a slogan reads: "Always a new Horizon." The Whit Walk was originally organised by the the Sunday School Union, now better known as the Christian Educational Council.

Cars everywhere in the restriction-free days of the early 1950s. The busy shoppers don't seem to care though, perhaps they had their mind on more exciting things, such as the impending coronation of her Majesty Queen Elizabeth II? This picture dates from June 1953 and shows the Swallows department store decked out in colourful decor in recognition of the big national celebration. The mock-tudor of the popular store was created to blend in with the older (though still 'mock') constructions adjacent to it. The store closed in 1970 and was demolished in 1973. The picture was taken from the corner of Elder Way (on the left) and the property on the left hand corner was Barclays Bank.

Below: An historic moment in the educational development of Chesterfield was captured in this photograph from 1956. The location of the event was the William Rhodes Secondary School and the occasion was a ground-breaking international exchange of teachers. Mr Boden from the William Rhodes School was sent to New Zealand and a teacher from that country, Mr Hall was engaged to work in Chesterfield for a year. The pupils of the school look very smart as they watch the introduction of their new teacher to Sir David Eccles, the visiting Minister of Education, overseen by the headmaster and the Mayor. One teacher at the school during this period recalls how the news of the forthcoming arrival of the New Zealand teacher was met by some of the younger boys. Many of them wanted to know if he was a Maori! Notice the photographer from the local press; he was as well-turned out as the subjects he had come to photograph with his crude, but effective camera and flash.

LANCASTER & THORPE

BRADWELL BRO

> ## "MAYOR-MAKING WAS USUALLY HELD IN MID-MAY AND ALWAYS ON A SUNDAY"

Above: Girl Guides formed part of this procession in the mid 1960s to mark the appointment of the latest Mayor of Chesterfield. "Mayor Making" was usually held in mid-May and always on a Sunday. In more recent years the event has not been quite as grand as it was here and modern Mayor-Making now occurs on Saturdays. This view of Knifesmithgate has not seen much physical change since the scene was recorded, though many of the retail businesses have changed hands. In the distance the faithful old Co-operative building is shown.

At leisure

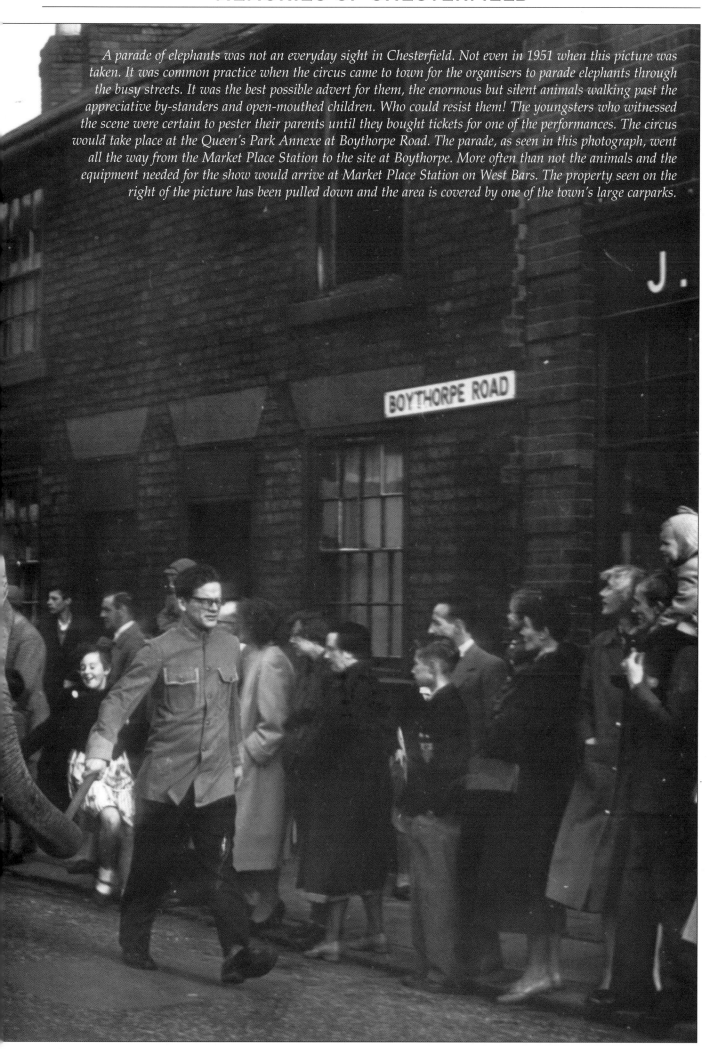

A parade of elephants was not an everyday sight in Chesterfield. Not even in 1951 when this picture was taken. It was common practice when the circus came to town for the organisers to parade elephants through the busy streets. It was the best possible advert for them, the enormous but silent animals walking past the appreciative by-standers and open-mouthed children. Who could resist them! The youngsters who witnessed the scene were certain to pester their parents until they bought tickets for one of the performances. The circus would take place at the Queen's Park Annexe at Boythorpe Road. The parade, as seen in this photograph, went all the way from the Market Place Station to the site at Boythorpe. More often than not the animals and the equipment needed for the show would arrive at Market Place Station on West Bars. The property seen on the right of the picture has been pulled down and the area is covered by one of the town's large carparks.

BOYTHORPE ROAD

Above: Few children would contest the view that the best place to be in the Chesterfield area, on a hot sunny day, was the Stand Road open-air swimming pool. This picture dates from over 60 years ago, in 1937. The facility certainly seems busy enough when this picture was taken and would have been a major attraction for the children of Whittington Moor and beyond.

Right: *Little brother* was not concerned at taking the pillion seat while his sister took command of this fine B.S.A motorcycle. A few years later and it would have been a different story! The photograph was taken near St. John's Road, Whittington Moor. Careful use of a magnifying glass reveals that the tax disc was due to expire in 1953, giving a fair indication of the date of the picture. The motorbike was probably their fathers' means of transport to and from work. It was a popular mode of transport at the time, the large capacity single-cylinder four-stroke engine providing a healthy mix of performance and economy. No one would have thought it in the 1950s, but the registration number on the bike - ORB 275 - would be much sought after in the present day by those trading in personalised number plates, and the bike highly prized by motorcycle enthusiasts as a collectors' item.

Left: A rather run-down view of Beetwell Street as it appeared at the dawn of the 1960s. Two young lads amuse themselves with this home-made trolley, constructed with parts from an old pushchair, a few planks and a fruit and vegetable case. Hours would be spent trying to locate a nut and bolt sturdy enough to act as the pivot on the front axle. We remember it well. The buildings towards the top of the picture were pulled down so that the modern Police Station could be built. All the properties on the right of Beetwell Street have been demolished over the years enabling the planners to create a road which is wider and straighter than shown here.

Above: The age of *romance* is captured in this photograph from 1960. The loving couple are about to mount the steps from the corner of St. Mary's Gate to St. Mary's Church. The War Memorial can be seen at the top of the picture. Beyond that level the path to Stephenson Place was to be found. This route was often used by people walking into town from the Midland Station. Perhaps this young lady had just met her 'young man' from that station when the picture was taken? Fashions of the day confirm the early '60s origin of the picture; the narrow trousers on the man and the seamed stockings and full floral dress on his young lady were typical of the time.

Below: The Odeon Cinema in Chesterfield could rightly lay claim to being one of the prettiest *Odeons* in the whole of Britain. This was the venue for many romantic meetings and first dates for the courting couples of the town and the photograph is certain to bring back happy memories for many readers of this book. It was a sad day for the town when, in 1981, the cinema closed. It later went on to be "The Winding Wheel" with a well-used function suite and lecture theatre. The establishment is located on Holywell Street near the Spire. This photograph was taken in 1956 and we believe that the film being shown at the time was *'The Battle of The River Plate.'*

Above: A picture certain to bring back memories, the old public baths building as it appeared in 1972. *The Corporation Slipper Baths* were a valued facility among local people in the days when most houses did not have a bath, and many did not even have running water. They date from 1900 and were located in South Place. The lovely old building is used as a craft centre as it approached its 100th birthday. In the right hand side of the background the old Courthouse building is visible. It was built in 1849 and pulled down in 1973. Chesterfield Bowling Club, one of the oldest in the country, had its club house beneath the Courthouse building and this obviously disappeared when the Courthouse was demolished. Their new Club house stands partly on the site of the old Courthouse.

CHESTERFIELD'S ODEON CINEMA COULD RIGHTLY LAY CLAIM TO BEING THE PRETTIEST ODEON IN THE COUNTRY"

On the move

A traffic accident at the Junction of Low Pavement was enough to draw the crowds when this picture was taken at 12.25 p.m on Wednesday October 18th 1939. The photograph was taken outside F. W Dutton's the chemists. The overturned motor car on the left of the picture looks dramatic, and it is a sobering thought to think that in the 1930s there were almost twice the number of traffic-related deaths on Britain's roads than there are today. This despite there being only a small fraction of the number of vehicles on the roads compared to modern times. The photograph provides yet another good reason, if one were needed, why it is a good thing that Chesterfield's inner shopping area is free of motors. The picture was taken just one month into the first phase of the Second World War. October saw the sinking of H.M.S Royal Oak with the loss of 810 lives at Scapa Flow.

"GEORGE STEPHENSON LIVED NEAR CHESTERFIELD FOR MANY YEARS AND IS BURIED AT TRINITY CHURCH"

Below: A grand exhibition was organised to commemorate the centenary of George Stephenson at the Market Place Station in 1948. This marvellous picture shows the engine named Stephenson with queues of people waiting for their chance to stand on the footplate. The powerful machine was a Patriot Class 4-6-0 engine built in the 1930s. George Stephenson, originally a native of Newcastle, lived at Tapton House for many years and is buried at Trinity Church. Market Place Station was on West Bars, near the Portland Hotel.

Above: Looking like some modern classic car rally, this scene along Low Pavement, facing New Square actually dates from 1958. All the buildings in this picture were extensively modernised at the end of the 1970s, though their facades were kept generally intact. There was much clearance to the rear of these properties along New Beetwell Street in order to build the major shopping precinct which now stands there. The buildings featured here are now referred to as "The Pavements" by local people.

Above: An evocative picture from 1963 featuring Chesterfield's Central Station shortly before it closed for good. The mainly timber construction looks quaint and attractive to us now, though no doubt it would have been rather draughty and daunting to maintain for the station staff who worked there. The station opened in 1882 on the line from Lincolnshire, Sheffield and Manchester, becoming part of the Great Central Railway in 1897. Like so many railway stations in the early 1960s it closed to passengers in 1963 and was demolished in 1967. As a point of interest, construction work seen in the background relates to the building of the College of Technology extension.

Left: It was common practice at one time to send basket loads of racing pigeons to far-flung areas of Britain by rail. You can imagine from this picture how popular this was with the station staff! Chesterfield Midland Station was the location of this scene which was entitled "Freedom" by the photographer and something quite unprintable by the porter who had just allowed the birds to escape. Signal boxes and the semaphore signals on the right have all disappeared now.

Bottom right: A familiar face at Chesterfield Central Station throughout the period when steam engines reigned supreme and no one would ever have imagined that the town could manage without the popular rail facility. This was Mr Ashton - he had spent many years as a porter at the station and this picture was taken in 1963 when the station was about to close forever. Mr Ashton is seen in nostalgic mood, looking at the station sign and contemplating his impending retirement. Let's hope he enjoyed a happy one.

Below: A sense of numbness was beginning to set in on the day that the Central Station closed in March 1963. Of course, the Dual Carriageway now runs along the track bed, enabling modern motorists to see this very view of the Crooked Spire as they travel towards the town centre. Anyone with the slightest interest in nostalgia or fondness for the town of Chesterfield cannot fail to be moved by this scene. Even the distinctive gas lamps with their lever-arms (used to turn on the gas supply) evoke powerful memories.

Right: This is an historic photograph, with special significance for anyone interested in railways and the development of transport systems in Chesterfield. It was taken on March 3rd 1963, the day that Chesterfield's Central Station closed. An army of railway-buffs descended to witness the departure of the last passenger train from the station, most of them equipped with cameras and a plentiful supply of film. Many would leave the station with a tear in their eye as they reflected on happier times and enjoyable excursions which began from these platforms. Of course, all this has gone now, and the age of the road has transformed this area with the arrival of the broad Dual Carriageway which follows the old track bed from Horns Bridge to Whittington Moor. At least the name lives on in the name of the modern motor route - Great Central Way.

Above: Chesterfield Midland Station as it appeared in 1964. The station has seen many changes since it was built in 1870. The first station in this locality was built in 1841, 100yds to the south of the present station. At one time Chesterfield had three busy stations, and Chesterfield Midland is the last one remaining, serving the busy London main line. The section with the three chimneys and the low building to the right have been removed and replaced with a modern structure. Modern parking bays and tastefully planted trees add to the appeal of the new station layout.

Around the town centre

Below: Around half a century has passed since this scene was recorded along Knifesmithgate. The photograph dates from 1954 and provides us with a delightful glimpse of ordinary life going on along this popular street. Swallow's department store can be seen on the right of the picture in all its mock-tudor splendour. On the left, more of this tudor style can be seen in the form of the 1920s properties which housed the Victoria Cinema, a billiard hall, a cafe, and a very popular ballroom. These have all since been converted to shop premises. The photo-graph affords another pleasant view of the 'crooked spire.' Shortly before this photograph was taken - in 1950 - the structure was the subject of extensive repairs. The top 40 feet required new timber and lead cladding to keep it in a safe condition. At the same time, the builders took the precaution of renovating the weather vane.

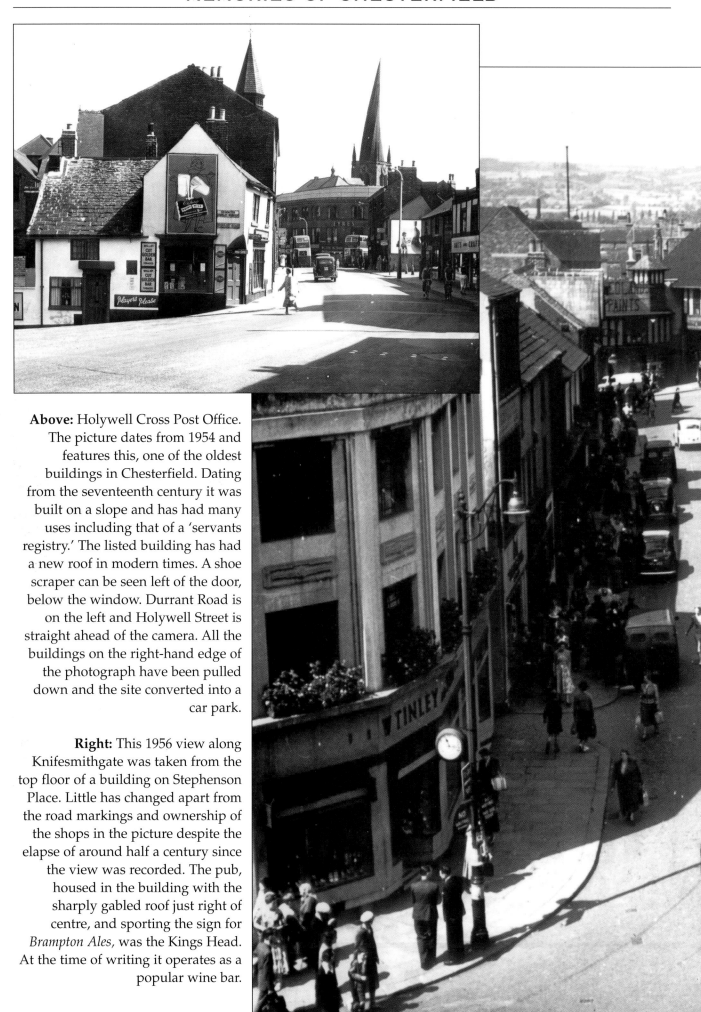

Above: Holywell Cross Post Office. The picture dates from 1954 and features this, one of the oldest buildings in Chesterfield. Dating from the seventeenth century it was built on a slope and has had many uses including that of a 'servants registry.' The listed building has had a new roof in modern times. A shoe scraper can be seen left of the door, below the window. Durrant Road is on the left and Holywell Street is straight ahead of the camera. All the buildings on the right-hand edge of the photograph have been pulled down and the site converted into a car park.

Right: This 1956 view along Knifesmithgate was taken from the top floor of a building on Stephenson Place. Little has changed apart from the road markings and ownership of the shops in the picture despite the elapse of around half a century since the view was recorded. The pub, housed in the building with the sharply gabled roof just right of centre, and sporting the sign for *Brampton Ales*, was the Kings Head. At the time of writing it operates as a popular wine bar.

Left: A view of the Shambles recorded around half a century ago. This dark passageway just yards away from Chesterfield's town centre was the home of the Royal Oak public house. The precise date when the picture was taken is uncertain, but believed to be sometime in the late 1940s.

stretch of road and pavement would have been familiar territory to anyone visiting patients at the old hospital.

Eventually the hospital was found to be inadequate for modern needs and a new one was developed at Calow. Thankfully the building remains, and has been tastefully cared for and renovated by the Kenning organisation, much to the approval of those who were once cared for here. The Belisha Beacons take their name from the Minister of Transport (Mr Hore Belisha) who was in in office at the time of the Road Traffic Act which introduced them.

> "THE ROYAL HOSPITAL WAS EVENTUALLY CLOSED AND A NEW ONE WAS DEVELOPED AT CALOW"

Above: A snowy afternoon in 1954 prompted the creation of this photograph to record the scene along Holywell Street. The picture is set opposite the Royal Hospital near the crossing on Holywell Street. This

Saltergate, looking east to Holywell Cross. The road on the right foreground is Elder Way and the picture dates from 1965. On the right, the large building behind the concrete lamp standard is still there at the time of writing, but all the buildings on the side of the post nearer the camera have been cleared. Another car park occupies the site. Dobbs Yard is the narrow passage standing between the stone cottages and the white building on the left of the scene. The yard was known as "Bedlam Yard" at one time because of the intense noise that was associated with it. This noise came from a combination of the chattering made by the stocking-knitting machines along the passage and the racket made by French prisoners of war lodged there during the Napoleonic War period.

Right: This picture was taken to record the intro-duction of the new roundabout at West Bars, looking towards Wheatbridge Road. The well-known Robinson works and local brewery is featured. The date of the photograph was August 1964. Adverts in the hoardings in the background promote the sale of Skol, Turog, Ovaltine and Players cigarettes. It might just be the elevated angle of the photograph, but the roundabout appears to have a strange service road within it leading to the flower beds in the centre. We wonder whether this would have been confusing to the motorists travelling round the island at times. There seem to plenty of arrows around the island to ensure that motorists would "keep left." Finally, note the Ford Thames van in the bottom right corner of the picture. The extra wide custom-built body suggests that it was being used as a mobile shop.

Left: A scene dominated by the simple but dignified lines of the Hippodrome. It dates from 1960, shortly before the Hippodrome was pulled down. Many Chesterfield folk will have fond memories of the walk along Corporation Street - either en-route to the Midland Station, seen to the right in this view or, better still, to meet a loved-one for an evening of entertainment. Also featured here is the Station Hotel, later to be re-named the 'Chesterfield Hotel.' The low building which housed Bowers Taxis has been pulled down since this photograph was taken, as have the premises of Pilkington's Motors. The Hippodrome was originally the Theatre Royal, but changed its name in 1912. Many national stars, including Gracie Fields and Sandy Powell appeared there, but the age of television and bingo caused its decline, closure and eventual demolition. Buildings to the right of the picture were later pulled down too, and the scene is unrecognisable at the time of writing, with a deep cutting containing a dual carriageway running right through it.

Right: This characterful Hillman Minx saloon is seen parked opposite Market Place Station - itself just visible on the left of the picture. This area along West Bars has now changed almost beyond recognition. All the buildings on the left were pulled down in the 1960s though the properties on the right of the picture remain in place at the time of writing. Arnold Lavers timber yard can be seen in the centre of this photograph and the station Goods Depot is shown on the right. The railway was always known locally as the East Coast Railway because it was intended to go through to Manchester. In the event it never got further than Chesterfield. The demolition, as already described, was conducted in order to make way for the construction of the A.G.D building.

Left: Many changes have taken place along Beetwell Street since this photograph was taken in the late 1950s. Road widening and demolition in the early 1960s altered the appearance of the street almost beyond recognition, though all the buildings on the left of the picture, behind the curvaceous Austin saloon, remain. Notice the couple walking away from the camera on the right. They are about to pass an old bow-window denoting the position of Chesterfield's best known clog maker, "Cloggie" Nash. Countless thousands of clogs were made, sold and repaired from these modest premises over a period of decades. Further still along the street there once stood a bakery. In the first half of this century the baker offered an unusual service that may be remembered by some local people. During hot weather, when it was uneconomic and inconvenient to light domestic fires for baking or heating, mothers would send their children to school along the street and have them call at the bakery with dough that they had prepared. The children would then call back on the way home from school and collect bread from the bakery which had been baked in the bakers' oven. All for the modest charge of a halfpenny.

Below: Holywell Cross as it looked in the early 1960s. Saltergate goes off to the left of the picture and Holywell Street goes off to the right, leading towards Sheffield Road. The character of this part of town has changed beyond recognition. All the buildings have been pulled down and the area is now dominated by a large car park and the one-way system. Damm's grocery store can be seen on the corner of the picture with a tripe shop on the left, and all formed part of a popular shopping area before the age of the supermarket took serious hold. In the shopping parade to the left of the bus was Burton's the tailor, established here in the year 1900. The tall building beyond the bus was Glossop's - it was constructed and opened in 1888. The white building on the extreme right housed a well-known local company, Thompson's Provision Factors. The area is believed to have taken its name from a cross which stood on the corner up until the turn of the century. No trace of the cross remains today.

Above: Part of the north side of New Square. At one time three hotels faced this part of the square. The Market Hotel, seen here, is the only one left. This photograph was taken in 1961. Chesterfield Valet Service on the corner of Soresby Street closed many years ago, the next occupant, Dawsons Curtains and Fabrics moved the shop front back around 3ft. At the time of writing Venus Shoes are located here now... and the shop front is back in its original position.

Long before the days when every policeman had a personal radio linking him to the station there used to be police telephone points dotted around the route of their beat. One can be seen here, in front of the hotel doorway, complete with light on top which was intended to catch the eye of passing bobbies when the station needed to contact them in an emergency. There were no obvious parking restrictions here - save the makeshift billboard outside the pub proclaiming 'no parking.'

The Mellors ice cream stand appears to be doing a brisk trade in the freshly made ice cream which was prepared at their works in Wards Yard near the Market Place.

Below: This photograph dates from the 1960s and shows Holywell Street, looking in an easterly direction. All buildings on the right of the picture have been pulled down, cleared in the 1970s in the drive to modernise the town and improve local communications. The tall dark building is Glossops - built in 1888, with Thompsons Provision Factors to the right of it. The Post Office on the left hand edge of the picture remains at the time of writing. Just to the right of the scene, and sadly out of view, was the location of another shop which was very popular. It was known as "Dollys" and gained a reputation for being open all hours - even on a Sunday - and for selling virtually everything you could need in the course of everyday life. "Dollys" was ahead of its time in this respect, for this was long before the days of the conve-nience store and off-licence on every street corner of the suburbs. Everyone in Chesterfield knew Dolly, but sadly Dolly and the shop have long since gone.

> "DOLLY'S WAS A POPULAR SHOP WHICH GAINED A REPUTATION FOR BEING OPEN ALL HOURS - A CONCEPT UNHEARD OF AT THE TIME"

The corner of Knifesmithgate and Broad Pavement as it appeared in September 1966. We can fix the picture in time even more precisely than this, for the clock on the left of the picture (Hodgsons) tells us that the picture was taken at 11.04 pm. Dominating the scene is the King's Head public house, purveyors of Warwicks ales from this mock-tudor building. The establishment is now a wine bar. Beyond the King's Head the Gas Showrooms can be seen and, far left, the *Swallow's* department store. A selection of delightful (mainly British) motor cars completes the picture.

Above: A very pleasant picture from the mid 1950s, the centrepiece of which is the Rural District Council Office. The establishment now goes under the name "North East Derbyshire Council Offices" and since the picture was taken the property has been extended by as least as much again to the right. This required the removal of the property seen here which once stood on that site. The road in the foreground is Saltergate and the grassed area between the position of the camera and the small van is now, what else, but a car park. The church on the right is the Church of the Annunciation (on Spencer Street) and the one visible on the left corner is the Cross Street Baptist Chapel.

Right: Packers Row, looking north to Burlington Street in a picture taken in 1964. The road to the left by the lamp standard is Central Pavement. The lamp itself is well-known and of historic interest. It dates from 1824 and was Chesterfield's first gas lamp. Early last century it stood on the south east corner of the Market Place outside Bettison's shop. All the property on the right of this picture has been pulled down and rebuilt. Turners was a very popular department store and Cantors was once an old stage coaching inn, going under the name of "Ye Olde Angel" with its gated entrance to the stables next to Turners.

Holywell Cross Post Office is featured in this photograph, taken in February 1964. It was, and still is an early seventeenth century building which has seen various uses over the years. It is possible to see the modification in the building line, between the advertising boards on the right of the main window of the Post Office. The facility closed as a Post Office in 1985 when houses to the rear were demolished and the Hospital (seen on the left) moved to Calow. The boarded door by the fall pipe led to a small yard. In recent times the building found use as a restaurant, named the 'Old Post' and its architectural importance was reflected in its status as a Listed Building.

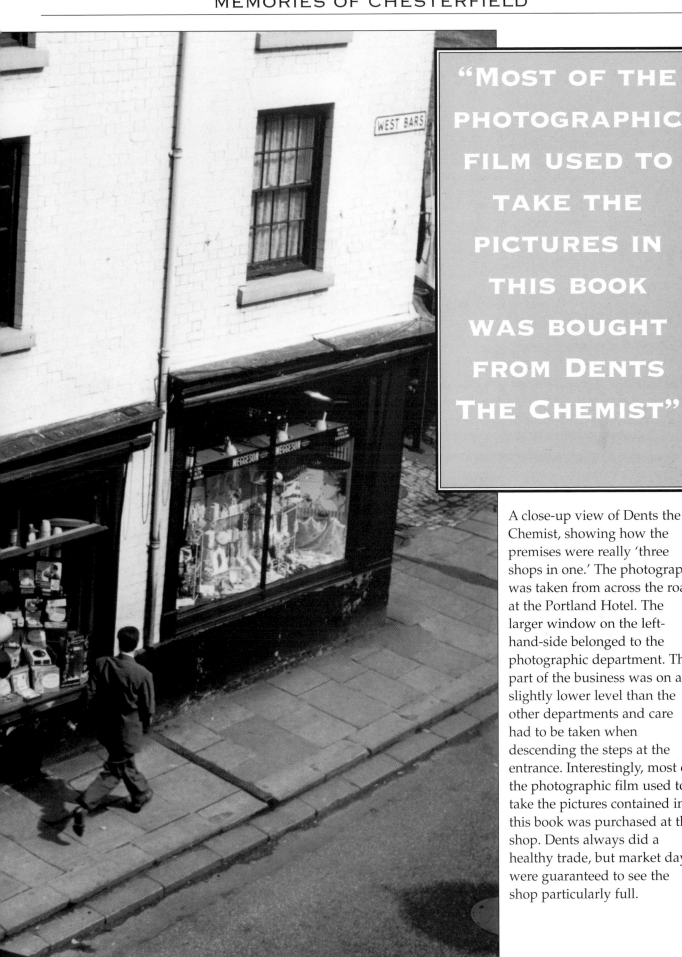

"MOST OF THE PHOTOGRAPHIC FILM USED TO TAKE THE PICTURES IN THIS BOOK WAS BOUGHT FROM DENTS THE CHEMIST"

A close-up view of Dents the Chemist, showing how the premises were really 'three shops in one.' The photograph was taken from across the road at the Portland Hotel. The larger window on the left-hand-side belonged to the photographic department. This part of the business was on a slightly lower level than the other departments and care had to be taken when descending the steps at the entrance. Interestingly, most of the photographic film used to take the pictures contained in this book was purchased at this shop. Dents always did a healthy trade, but market days were guaranteed to see the shop particularly full.

Above: A familiar view of a once-busy route through the town. The picture dates from 1960 and features, of course, Horns Bridge. Most of what can be seen in this photograph has disappeared to make way for a huge roundabout. Lordsmill Street is in the foreground and Derby Road can be seen on the right. Hasland Road runs to the left. Below the brick road-arch in the distance part of an advertising poster can be seen, and along the way to the right was a row of terraced houses known as Central Terrace.

Below: A remarkable picture guaranteed to evoke feelings of nostalgia in the heart of everyone who witnessed the scene at the time. Central to the photograph is the temporary chalet building which housed Dents chemists shop while the firm was waiting for its new store to be completed. The popularity of Dents meant that the chalet was frequently overcrowded - not a place for those prone to claustrophobia. When Dents' new premises opened the company donated the chalet to the hospital for use as a nurses' rest room. The beautiful lamp standard is worth a mention. How much nicer it looks than the concrete examples most towns erect today, and well done *Chesterfield* for preserving several of these older lamps at various points in the town for us to enjoy and admire today. Beyond the lamp in this picture is the National Westminster Bank, later (in 1968) to be replaced with a modern bank building.

Left: A mid-1960s family outing to the shops was the subject of this picture. It actually dates from 1964 and shows the figures ambling towards Market Place with Burlington Street to the left. Packers Row is ahead, leading to South Street. Two first floor bay windows can be seen at the top of the picture - they mark the location of the popular Burlington Cafe which operated above a grocers shop on the street. Packers row and the area of narrow passages to the right is probably the oldest part of the town, known as the Shambles, the home of the half-timbered Inn the *Royal Oak*. At the time of writing the buildings on the right are still in place, but on the left all the ones on the left have been pulled down and the distant (set back) properties have been rebuilt.

Above: A 1950s view of High Street with Glumangate on the right, behind the man walking towards the camera. Sadly, all the properties, with the exception of the Midland Bank, have been swept away, the area now being dominated by Littlewood's huge department store. Perhaps the most interesting structure in this scene is the arched building facing Market Place. It was one of three similar-styled Regency structures. This was one of the properties which was cleared, two similar ones remain but have been extensively modified to meet modern requirements. The arched building featured here was once the retail premises from where T.P. Woods ran his wines and spirits store. The business was established in 1844. Finally we should not leave this picture without mention of the shop seen on the right. Maxwell's was the ladies outfitters where hundreds of Chesterfield brides purchased their wedding gowns over a period lasting decades. Mothers would often bring their daughters to the store to sample the quality and service that they had enjoyed when they had married... and so it went on.

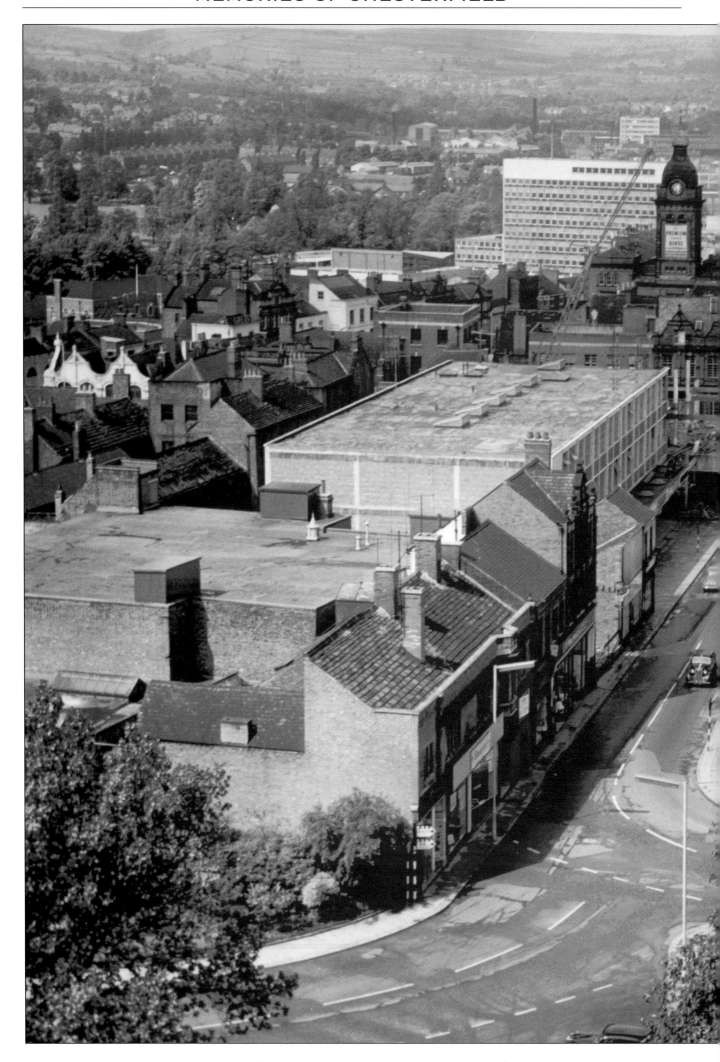

An elevated view of the centre of Chesterfield which dates from 1964. The photograph was taken from the base of the spire of the Parish Church, looking in the direction of Burlington Street, now a busy pedestrian precinct. In the centre of the scene a new shop and office development can be seen. It had only recently been completed. The property next to it, nearer to the camera, was later to be improved and developed by Woolworths. In the distance, the dark tower, complete with with clock and dome denotes the location of the Market Hall. To the left of it, the modern white structure is the A.G.D building. Who could have guessed, in 1964, that its presence on the skyline would have been so short lived? The light-coloured building on the right of the Market Hall is Dents the chemists.

"THE MARKET HALL WAS BUILT FOR A PRIVATE COMPANY IN 1857 AND WAS TAKEN OVER BY THE CORPORATION IN 1873"

January 1964, and an elevated view of Chesterfield looking across New Square, past the Market Hall towards High Street and the 'crooked spire.' The Market Hall was built for a private company in 1857 and taken over by the Corporation in 1873. The acquisition of market companies by local councils was typical of the years towards the end of the nineteenth century. The building was renovated and extended in 1976/7. On the left can be seen the Market Hotel and other shops, along with the Post Office which opened in 1866. Initially the Post Office was situated across the road in the Market Hall. Beyond the Post Office was the Westminster Bank. It was constructed in 1894 and pulled down in 1968. A modern structure stands in its place.

An impressive aerial view of Chesterfield showing some of the changes that have affected the town over the years. As a point of reference, the 230 ft crooked spire of St. Mary's Church can be seen on the centre-right of the photograph with the Town Hall above and beyond it. The larger part of the existing church building dates from the 14th Century, though Chesterfield had a church dating back to Norman times. Much has been written about the steeple and its shape which has helped make Chesterfield famous throughout the country. It is now generally accepted that it is the heat of the sun that has caused the warping of the timbers enclosed within it and the lead cladding which covers them. Modern visitors are often surprised to learn than the spire has had this appearance for several hundred years, and that nearly every spire with this wood and lead construction has a tendency to bend to the south-west.

"R.W. PROCTER HAD NURSERIES ALONG ASHGATE ROAD AS WELL AS THE LOW PAVEMENT PREMISES"

Low Pavement and the junction with Park Road are featured in this photograph from the 1960s. The firm known as R.W Proctor, Florists, Landscape Gardeners and Seed Merchants (established in 1825) dominates the picture. They had nurseries along Ashgate Road as well as this outlet. The cute Austin A35 van adds character to the scene. The registration plate, *8230R* would be worth a fortune now!

Wartime

Below: During the run up to the start of the last war, and, indeed, throughout it, it was impossible to be too young to help in the preparations. This picture looks like one from an Enid Blyton story but in actual fact this 'famous four' was undertaking the very serious job of distributing gas masks to the outlying farms around Sheepbridge. The precise location is Dunston Lane and the children concerned were (left to right) Phyllis Slack, Mary Boyes, Dorothy Williamson, and Margaret Slack.

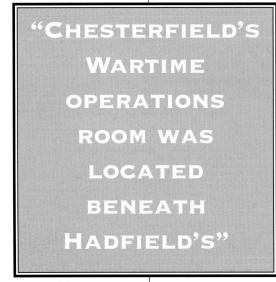

"CHESTERFIELD'S WARTIME OPERATIONS ROOM WAS LOCATED BENEATH HADFIELD'S"

Right: An historic picture taken as the preparations for war reached their peak in Chesterfield. The 'operations room' was located underground, beneath the Hadfields Shop, along High Street a location chosen because of the belief that it would afford some protection from an enemy air-raid. The chairs were positioned near the six telephones intended to be used to direct various departments of the Council, the Police, Fire Brigade and A.R.P in the event of a heavy bombing raid or other disruptive situation. It was intended that all matters relating to public health and public order would be managed from here.

Left: A proud father poses for the camera with his latest arrival. The baby had not arrived from Mars, in fact the 'arrival' was not a baby at all, but an anti-gas attack suit which was compulsory for babies in the United Kingdom during the Second World War. An air pump at the side of the suit enabled anxious parents to replenish the supply of air to the precious package inside. It is said that most babies were less than enthusiastic abut the prospect of being encased in the suit - and who could blame them? The picture was taken in 1939. In the event there was never any gas attack on British soil during the course of the Second World War.

Right: A photograph from around 1940 records the impressive buttress of sandbags laid to protect the Town Hall from the blast of an enemy bombing raid. The mountain of sandbags cannot fail to impress the observer in modern times, and the wartime feel of the photograph is made complete by the saloon car pictured on the right. Notice the white-painted wing-edges of the car - a seemingly crude attempt to achieve some semblance of visibility during the blackout.

Top right: This is not a picture of an all-male early barbecue party. The purpose of the gathering was far more serious than that - and much harder work too. The scene is set at the St. Mary Swanwick School at Old Whittington in September 1940. The picture was taken soon after the *Battle of Britain* and features some of the parents filling sandbags designed to afford protection to people and property in the even of an enemy bombing raid. At the time this picture was taken the Blitz was taking place in London and it was only three months since the evacuation had taken place at Dunkirk. Against this background it is not surprising that the task of protecting the area against the Nazis was being taken very seriously.

Bottom right: A welcome rest from the job of digging a trench for an air-raid shelter at St. Mary Swanwick School. The picture dates from September 1940. Parents, teachers and some of the older pupils had volunteered for the work which was given added urgency by news of the first raids on London by the enemy bombers. The concept of exploiting voluntary help from a variety of sources would become key to the nation's success during the war. Britain was operating under a siege economy, unlike Germany, with an unprecedented degree of state control and involvement in the daily lives of her citizens. The fields around Chesterfield saw members of the *Land Army* engaged in food production - there were 80,000 women throughout Britain doing similar work as the country sought increasingly innovative ways of beating the enemy. In Germany rations were comparatively high, taxes relatively low and women never fully mobilised to help in the war effort.

Above: This interesting picture features a parade on Queen's Park in wartime. The Mayor of Chesterfield can be seen taking the salute on the stand decorated with several Union Flags. The photograph was taken on 25th August 1942. Queen's Park was created by public subscription and opened to celebrate Queen Victoria's Golden Jubilee in 1887. The generosity of Alderman T.P Wood is closely associated with the fundraising efforts which resulted in the opening of the park. Alderman Wood was first elected to the Council in 1863 and was appointed Mayor in 1873. During his term of office the Corporation also bought the Market Company in Chesterfield.

Right: A group of *Chesterfield Local Defence Volunteers* are pictured in the early 1940s. The contribution made by voluntary organisations during the Second World War cannot be overestimated. The Womens Voluntary Service, later to become the Womens Royal Voluntary Service, played an important role in the support of the war effort on the Home Front, as did many other organisations. In May 1940 the Local Defence Volunteers was formed, later to become known as the Home Guard. Local appeals were made for Auxiliary Fire and Ambulance personnel, along with Air Raid Wardens and associated voluntary groups. War had broken out on September 3rd 1939 and the evacuation of children from likely air-raid targets began immediately. A staggering 1.5 million children were evacuated, a tremendous logistical exercise. By 1940, when the feared bombing had failed to materialise the children were returned home. Gas masks were issued to every man, woman and child in the U.K and people were required to carry them with them at all times.

Below: Goldwell Hill was the scene chosen by the photographer for this picture. Captured on camera is Chesterfield's very own Home Guard consisting of gents who were too old, too unfit or too young for the 'call-up', or members of reserved occupations. The Home Guard was intended to be Britain's final line of defence in the event of an enemy invasion and trained relentlessly to ensure that they would be prepared for 'anything' if the worst came to the worst. This picture was taken soon after 1940 and shows the proud, upright soldiers, complete with enthusiastic young supporters, marching perfectly in-step up Goldwell Hill, Ashgate.

"THE TOWN HALL'S DECORATIONS ON V.E. DAY REFLECTED THE RELIEF, JOY AND SHEER JUBILATION FELT BY CHESTERFIELD"

held celebrations to mark the 1000th anniversary of its foundation. By this time it was a town of 70,000 people, having grown remarkably from a population of just 5000 in little over 100 years.

Above: The Town Hall was in victorious mood when this picture was taken. It dates from the night of May 8th 1945 and the decorations reflect the intensity of the relief, joy and sheer jubilation felt in Chesterfield and beyond on the news that the Germans had surrendered. The Town Hall building dates from 1938. Chesterfield grew up around the Roman road which came from *Little Chester* through Chesterfield to Templeborough (near Rotherham) and on to York. The first 'modern' Chesterfield mayor was Ralf Clark who took on the role in the reign of Queen Elizabeth I in 1598. By 1951 the town

Below: *Loco Terrace,* Hasland was the location of this photograph from 1945. The occasion was one of the scores of street parties which were held in Chesterfield, as in the rest of Britain, to mark the end of the war in Europe. Facing the camera, from the left: June Staton, Brenda Towers, Alan Mee, Rita Williams, Ivy Ashton, Iris Hullet, George Harrison, Cyril Jones, Kenneth Williams and Joe Speed. With their backs to the camera we see: Frank Hullet, Mr. Hullet, Bernice Hullet, Maurice Hullet and Mrs. Hullet.

"SCORES OF STREET PARTIES WERE HELD ON V.E. DAY IN CHESTERFIELD AND THE REST OF BRITAIN"

Above: A delightful group photograph dating from 1945 and featuring mainly young children with their mothers along with one or two older children in attendance. Sadly the names of the smiling subjects are not known to us - though we would be pleased to hear from anyone who could enlighten us here - but we do know the cause of the happy expressions. The picture was taken as part of the celebrations to mark Victory in Europe. The participants were all residents in the Stand Road area of Whittington Moor.

This historic Chesterfield gathering of over half a century ago was captured on camera for us to admire today. The photograph was taken as hundreds gathered on Market Place to rejoice, give thanks and celebrate the end of the Second World War. Of course, for many present here the celebration was tinged with deep sadness and thoughts of loved ones who had made the ultimate sacrifice to overcome the Nazi tyranny. The date was May 8th 1945. All the Services were represented, including the Home Guard and other Civil Defence, Church and Youth organisations. Of course, it would

be many weeks and even months before surviving members of the victorious armed forces would be demobbed and return home. And years before we would see the end of rationing and the return to normal daily life. Note the water fountain, known as 'the pump' which stood in the Market Place, slightly left of centre towards the top of the picture. This was often used as a makeshift platform from which speakers would address anyone prepared to listen. It is said the John Wesley preached from this spot in the year 1777.

Above: An historic picture from May 1945. Emotions were running high as the celebrations to mark the end of the war were well under way. The photograph was taken, of course, along Knifesmithgate, on V.E day itself. Swallows department store is just out of sight on the right and Taylors the chemists is visible at the top of the street. The picture was taken at 3.00 pm according to the clock on the crooked spire. The mock tudor buildings are decorated for the end of war festiv-ities. Other shops featured here include the Scotch Wool and Hosiery Stores on the left. The queue for ices on the left of the picture reflects the fact that it was a warm sunny day. People on the street would have been swelled with excitement at the thought of how their lives would be transformed by the end of the war.

All change

Below: Horns Bridge is featured in this delightful picture from around 1960. The motorcar in the scene - a Ford Prefect - is rather older than this. On the left of the picture the Horns Hotel with its distinctive and ornate architecture can be seen beside the parade of highly shaded shops. This is another example of a part of Chesterfield which has undergone a dramatic and near total change over a relatively short period of time. The high level bridge which carried the railway line from the Market Place Station on West Bars to the East Coast has been demolished. Indeed, every structure in this scene, with the sole exception of the 'girder' bridge behind the motor car, has been cleared since this picture was taken. In modern times a large roundabout was built to join the Great Central Way at this location.

Main picture: This is how Chesterfield's skyline appeared in 1950. The foreground features the playground of Hipper Junior School, the thoroughfare beyond it being Markham Road which went on to join Lordsmill Street to the right. Advertising hoardings can be seen just below the centre of the picture. A builders' yard stood just behind them with a shop to the left. Yet another large roundabout was created at the Lordsmill Street junction, and the builders' yard along with all the property behind it, was cleared to make way for the Tax Office, Social Security Offices, shops and a bingo hall. Hipper Street Junior School later became the offices of the Centre for Community Education.

Left: A picture from 1974 showing the Markham Road and Lordsmill Street round-about. Hipper Street School became the Teachers Centre and most of the playground was absorbed in order to improve the road layout in the area. The Tax Office is the dominant modern building in this picture, it was built on what was formerly a builders' yard. The flat-roofed building in the foreground is a tyre and exhaust centre and the distinctive crooked spire of the Parish Church, sandblasted in 1973, dominates the Chesterfield skyline.

Top right: This view was captured from outside the Post Office, looking across New Square to West Bars. The Market Hall is on the left of the picture and it was the construction of that building which led to the re-naming of 'Swines Green' as New Square in recognition of the belief that the old name was inappropriate for an area so close to such a presti-gious local facility. The Market Hall was renovated and extended in 1979/80. The two tower cranes are worth a mention; the one on the left was being used to construct the A.G.D building and the one on the right was involved in the construction of the new Dents chemists' store. The buildings in the distance, behind the right-hand crane, have long since been pulled down and replaced by a modern building of abut five storeys.

Below: An unpleasant day during February 1962 saw preparations underway to demolish the much-loved Dents Chemists store. As the age of concrete and carparks dawned in Britain, Chesterfield had decided to erect a massive concrete shop and office development here. Courageously, Dents decided that they would remain open during the time of the development and elected to operate from a temporary 'chalet' building at the side of the original store. It is seen here under construction. During this period cars were allowed to park on the market area - at no cost - while the market stalls were unused. Interestingly, a large white box can be seen next to the traffic light in the picture. It is a relic of the age of electric trams - a junction box which enabled trams to divert into a waiting area in New Square. This, along with many other items of 'street furniture' in Chesterfield has long since disap-peared.

Below right: A very unusual view of Chesterfield Town Hall from the corner of Park Road, with Dents temporary 'chalet' on the right. The picture dates from 1962 and shortly after it was taken work began on the major task of excavating the founda-tions of the new building which would dominate this site. The white-coated figure here is the chemist and director of Dents, Mr Mark Evans. This area is now free from the danger and pollution of motor traffic.

Right: A view along Burlington Street, looking west, showing people going about their day-to-day business. The picture dates from 1961 and features the street part-way through the development which would transform it. The Beehive (Cussins) has gone, though one shop remains at the far end of the view. Two other retail properties, Rooths sweet shop and Dewhurst's the butchers traded successfully until the properties were absorbed into the Woolworths development. The properties on the right of the scene can still be seen at the time of writing, but they have changed hands several times since the picture was taken.

Left: A rare glimpse of Burlington Street from 1953 giving a good impression of just how busy the thoroughfare was at the time. The scene is certain to rekindle memories among older readers who were more familiar with the area in these days. All the buildings on the right of the picture, as far as, and including the one next to the bus, have been pulled down. The property on the right, seen propped up with heavy timbers (the technical term for which is "raking shores") was very old and originally the location of *The Beehive*. The top storey was removed for safety reasons shortly after this photograph was taken, but the lower floor remained in use until it too was pulled down in the early 1960s. Three large plate-glass windows can be seen on the first floor of the retail premises beside the bus in the picture. This was originally the location of Dobbs the ironmongers. Clever use of the upstairs windows represented an innovative marketing ploy on the part of the shrewd ironmonger. The busy tram, and later bus-route presented the opportunity to display a wide range of tempting products to the passengers on these vehicles as they stopped at the adjacent bus stop. Consequently the upstairs window of the shop acquired the same importance as the one on the ground floor.

Below: Perhaps an early hint of things to come, as pedestrians dominate this stretch of Burlington Street, long before the planners decided to ban motor vehicles from this area completely. The photographer was looking towards the west when he took the picture. Rooths and Dewhursts already looked rather isolated in the scene which dates from 1962.

Right: Burlington Street, looking east towards the spire in 1963. The photograph was taken to record the changes which had recently taken place here, including the new block on the right. Rooths and Dewhurst's shops were still trading from this location but the extension of Woolworths' frontage caused their closure a few years later. Exposed brickwork on the right hand edge of the property, beyond the new block, indicate a later development on the corner with Packers Row.

This stood on piers, extending forward to the original building line.

Below: Work in progress at the Markham Road extension is clearly in evidence in this picture. The scene dates from July 1963. The newly completed A.G.D building is clearly in view. The A.G.D building was expected to last a lot longer than the short life span it achieved, as a result of problems with the some of the material used to build it. The consequence was that it was completely demolished in 1997 and the 1000 people who worked there were relocated to another new building on Boythorpe Road.

Shopping

This happy scene was recorded at Chesterfield Market in 1938. It features a Patent Medicine Salesman hawking his wares from the top of a tea chest. Goodness only knows what his claims were for the substance in his little bottles. It's a frightening thought to consider the potential effects that the potions might have had on the unwary. Still, the onlookers here appear to be hard to impress, judging by the gloomy looks on their faces, and we would be surprised if any of them actually bought anything.

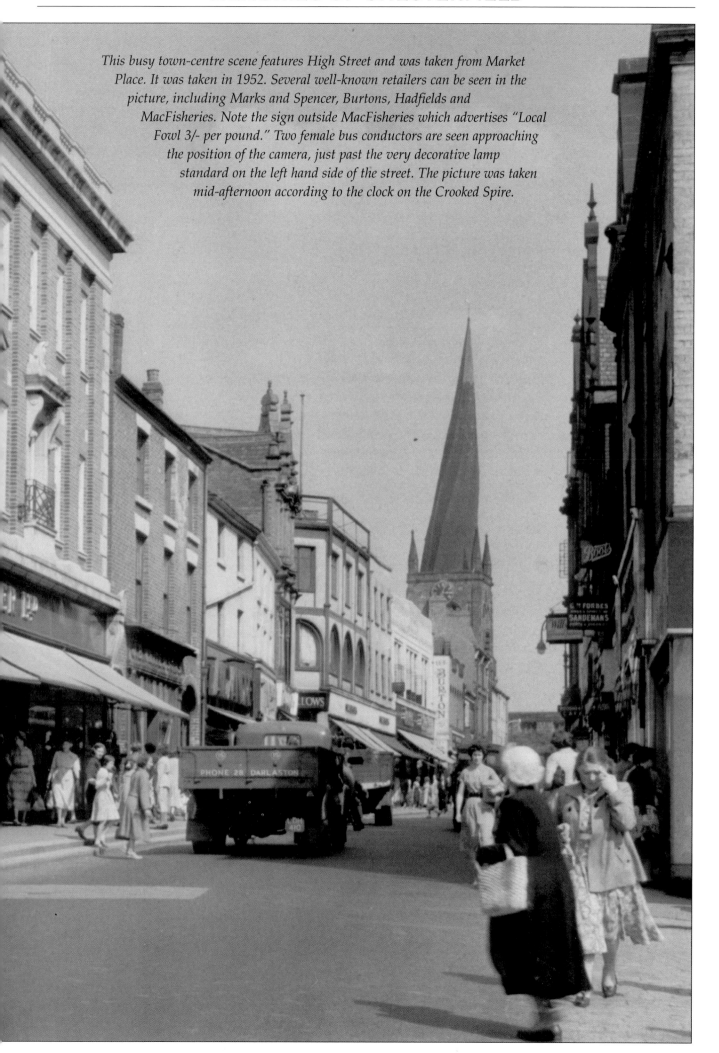

This busy town-centre scene features High Street and was taken from Market Place. It was taken in 1952. Several well-known retailers can be seen in the picture, including Marks and Spencer, Burtons, Hadfields and MacFisheries. Note the sign outside MacFisheries which advertises "Local Fowl 3/- per pound." Two female bus conductors are seen approaching the position of the camera, just past the very decorative lamp standard on the left hand side of the street. The picture was taken mid-afternoon according to the clock on the Crooked Spire.

This is how the High Street and Glumangate appeared to shoppers and visitors to the town in 1966. Pedestrians had to dodge the traffic in those days and endure the smell and health risks associated with their exhaust fumes. This picture recreates a charmingly nostalgic atmosphere. The small delivery vans about to drive past the Midland Bank look like toys to the modern eye, and the American-styled Vauxhall saloon approaching the position of the camera is guaranteed to bring back memories of carefree 1960s motoring to car enthusiasts. Beyond the Midland Bank other familiar businesses can be seen. Marks and Spencers, Snelsons and Boots. The Refuge Assurance Company offices were above the Midland Bank. The scene in this area of Chesterfield has changed dramatically with many of these buildings having been removed in order to create the site for the modern Littlewoods store which now dominates the location.

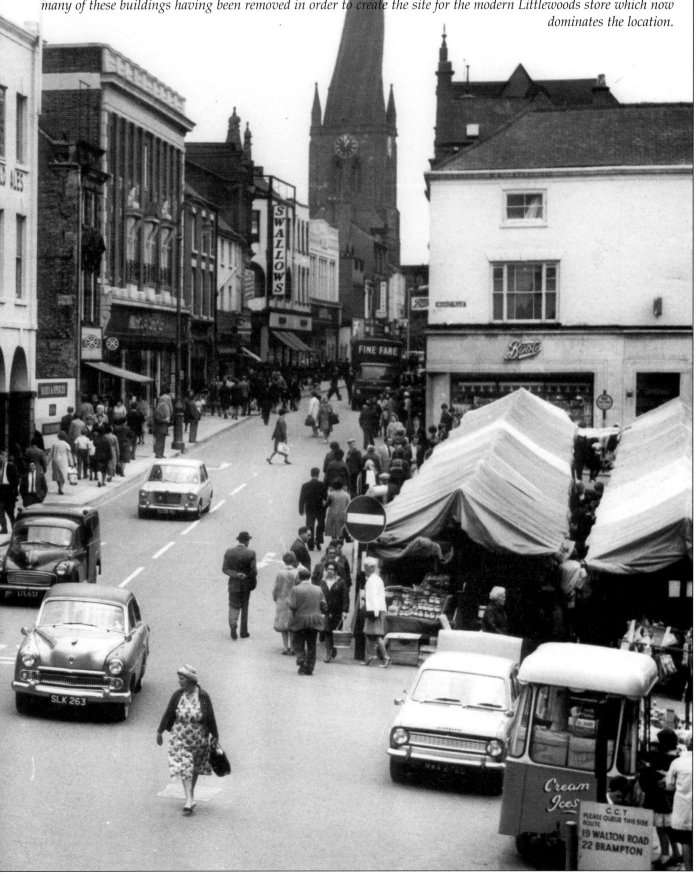

Below: This delightful picture was taken from the High Street (Market Place) looking west to New Square. Major alterations took place at the Market Hall between 1979 and 1980. It had been built in 1857 and has not always received the kindest comments about its design since that time. All the buildings on the right of this picture have been pulled down. The arches of T.P Woods (wines and spirits) were close to a passage which led to the popular King and Miller public house. The area is now dominated by the Littlewoods store. In the distance there is evidence of the 'old' meeting the 'new' with the massive tower crane helping the construction of the new Dents chemists shop, and the ornate lamp standard evoking memories of earlier times in the town.

Right: Many a memory will be stirred by this photograph of Hadfield and Sons, 'Pork and Provision Merchants' in Chesterfield between 1859 and 1965. Local people were sad to hear the news of their impending closure in 1965 after a presence in the town which lasted over a century. Occasionally old records can be found in Chesterfield which refer to an area called 'Hadfield Town.' This name relates to a bakery operated by the company featured here which was located in the Beetwell Street area many decades ago. The dominance of that bakery caused the area around it to become known as 'Hadfield Town.' MacFisheries on the right of this picture later moved when the site was required to form part of the Marks and Spencer store extension. This photograph was taken in 1965.

> "MAJOR ALTERATIONS TOOK PLACE AT THE MARKET HALL BETWEEN 1979 AND 1980"

Above: New Square in 1961. Last Century the area was known as "Swines Green" or the "Pig Market" and incorporated a small pond. There were no market stalls present in those days of course. The buildings in the background are extremely old. The dark building with the white rectangle was an old inn, the Star and Garter. At one time there were three inns serving New Square: The Peacock, The Star and Garter and the Market Hotel. The Star and Garter closed in 1937 but the Market Hotel remains. Much has been written about John Dent and the growth of his chemists business. Early records suggest that he dispensed his first prescription in January 1903. The old building shown here was pulled down in 1961. The new business incorporates many offices as well as the chemists and photography business, still run as a family firm almost a hundred years after it was established.

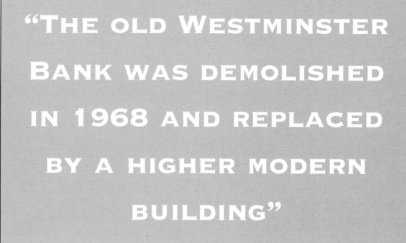

"THE OLD WESTMINSTER BANK WAS DEMOLISHED IN 1968 AND REPLACED BY A HIGHER MODERN BUILDING"

Below: New Square Market stalls were erected before and after market days and the areas used for car parking (which was free of charge in those days) in the interim. Work can be seen in progress here in the shadow of the Market Hall clock tower. The Market Hall on the right has been extended towards the camera during renovation. The buildings on the left remain at the time of writing with the exception of the centre building with the tall chimneys, the old Westminster Bank, demolished in 1968 and replaced by a higher modern building with modern design. The picture dates from 1953.

A photograph dating from 1956 showing High Street looking east. The Market and the shops featured here remain at the time of writing, though the first shop on the left, Burtons, has moved to Burlington Street, further along towards the spire. T.P. Woods with its arches and the shop beyond it have all been pulled down and replaced by the Littlewoods store. Marks and Spencers seen in the centre of this photograph, is still a dominant force in Chesterfield retailing at this location.

A delightful picture dating from 1961. Heavily-shaded stalls protect fresh produce and other tempting products from the the midday sun. The picture shows a typical day at the market with Dents Chemists in the background.
The market has always been an important part of Chesterfield's local economy. Over the years it has succeeded in attracting thousands of people into Chesterfield from the surrounding villages and towns, as well as providing a welcome source of bargain-priced goods for local people to buy.

At work

A photograph from 1966 which was clearly taken to record the appearance of the A.G.D building - the Accountant Generals Department of the Post Office. It had been standing for three years when this picture was taken but demolished in 1997 when serious problems with the fabric of the building were encountered. Keen eyes may just be able to discern the outline of the controversial piece of sculpture at the base of the building. The work is one by Barbara Hepworth. The Market Place Station can be seen on the left of the A.G.D building. It was pulled down soon after this scene was captured. The decision to site the A.G.D building in Chesterfield was welcome news for the area when it was announced in the early 1960s. Over 1000 staff were employed there and a new housing estate was built at Loundsley Green to accommodate them. In more recent times the demolition of the A.G.D building caused the staff to be moved to a new building on Boythorpe Road.

Above: When Princess Margaret visited the area in 1963 one of her engagements was at the Robinsons complex on Wheatbridge Road. In this photograph some of Robinsons former employees and the current workforce were seen leaving the area after lining the road outside the building. The industrial building featured on the far left was one of Robinsons and remains at the time of writing. The "Bold Rodney" public house has completely changed. It had taken its name from Admiral George Rodney who was born in Walton on Thames in 1718. He is famous for having gone to sea at the age of 12 and gaining the command of his own shop by the age of 24. His audacious acts of heroism led to him gaining the nickname "Bold Rodney." Regrettably the pub name has gone now and the building serves as a Chinese Restaurant.

Above right: Hipper Street South which leads to Markham Road, is captured in this very nostalgic view from 1964. Feelings of nostalgia are prompted by the presence of this delightful gas lamp which would have been taken for granted in the 1950s and '60s, but considered the centrepiece of many up-market domestic gardens in modern times. How times change! The large building on the right was known as Harrisons Boot and Shoe Warehouse. It was originally built in 1750 as a silk mill. It was pulled down in 1970 along with the houses seen on the left of it. The mill was powered for much of its early life by the River Hipper which formed a loop at this point. When water power was superseded the loop was cut out and the river course straightened. Silk Mill Yard, just to the other side of the mill housed much of the workforce. The mixture of 1960s motorcars and Morris half-ton van add to the nostalgic feel created by the photograph.

From George Kenning to the GK Group

GK Group Limited are Chesterfield and North Derbyshire's Main Ford Dealer. Based in Chatsworth Road, the business has sold Ford cars and vans as well as used vehicles and service and repair work for over eighty years.

The roots of GK Group go back over a hundred and twenty years to 1878 when Frank Kenning opened a hardware business in Clay Cross selling all sorts of goods, including kerosene, candles and petroleum products which resulted in a natural progression into the motor trade.

Frank's son, Sir George Kenning followed his father as head of the business and enthusiastically saw the possibilities of the new motor car trade. He gained the Ford franchise for Frank Kenning and Sons in 1915 and this was followed later with extensive distribution rights for Morris. One of Sir George's biggest deals was in 1927 when for £62,925 he bought the entire Morris factory production. In 1938 Kennings Limited became a public company and subsequent mergers and changes gradually gained Kennings' franchises for Austin, Morris, NIG, Standard, Triumph, Rover and Daimler cars.

After the war, growth was particularly marked. In 1950 there were fifty depots but by the time of Sir George's death in 1956, there were eighty. He was

Above: Sir George Kenning at the wheel of a 1931 Morris Minor Tourer.
Below: Frank Kenning originally opened a hardware business at Clay Cross as this turn of the century picture shows.

succeeded by his son, George as chairman and joint managing director together with his brother David.

The brothers dedicated themselves to expanding and modernising the Kenning Motor Group as it was now called and the business grew to 300 depots with interests in motor vehicles, fuel, car, and van rental and tyres with over 8,000 employees.

Above: Among the many unusual vehicles supplied by George Kenning were a fleet of one ton roadless lorries which went to Anglo-Persian Oil.
Right: Kenning Motor Group's former Head office at Manor Offices, Old Road, Chesterfield. This building now houses the Post Office's Information Technology Services.

The most notable acquisition was of the London Austin distributor, Car Mart which held the Royal Warrant for supply to HM Queen and a BMC import and distribution operation in Zimbabwe, formerly Southern Rhodesia.

Kenning Motor Group achieved great horizontal expansion using the synergy of their substantial

motor vehicle sales businesses. Kenning Tyres Services was developed to a national network, becoming one of the largest suppliers of car, commercial and earth mover tyres as well as operating three tyre remoulding factories marketing their own label, Fisk and John Bull tyres.

In addition to operating over 100 Petrol Forecourts, Kenning Motor Group built the Motorway Service sites at Strensham M5 and Anderton M61 and had an extensive fuel

distribution Company for Shell-Mex and BP. Vehicle building was another large side to the business with factories producing the famous three wheel W&E Electric milk float in Shrewsbury and Road Tankers in Ossett.

Kenning Car and Van Rental, with its highly visible rental vans, is perhaps one of the most well known of Kenning Companies. The Company were pioneers in the business, at the turn of the century horses were hired, mainly to BP and bicycles, mainly to Shell.

Above: An impressive line-up of Ford Zephyrs and Zodiacs from the 1960s with facing cars from Austin Morris.
Right: Kenning car Rental, an independent company since 1994, now has its Head Office in Durrant House, the former site of Chesterfield's Royal Hospital (built 1859), where it continues as one of the UK's largest car and van rental businesses and one of Chesterfield's largest employers.

Wadham Stringer to become Wadham Kenning.

In 1987, Sir George's grandsons, George, David and Richard - the fourth generation - established their own Company and bought out the Kenning Motor Group's Ford interests in Chesterfield and Sheffield renaming the Company GK Group, using their grandfather, George Kenning's initials. In the same year the new company bought the Ford

In 1954 they purchased 'Self Motoring Limited' specialists in short term hire. The business rapidly expanded with the acquisition of the Irish firm, Joe Malone Car Hire as well as the development of a business in France. In 1970 they were able to claim a hire fleet of 5000 vehicles.

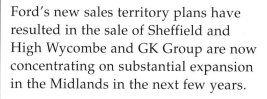

In 1981 George Kenning died unexpectedly and brother David died the following year. They were succeeded by Bart Oxspring and Jerry Foster. However in 1986 the Kenning Motor Group was subject to a take-over by Tozer, Kemsley and Millbourn, as a result the entity was divided up and the majority of assets were disposed of, though some of the franchised motor vehicle sales outlets merged with another TKM company,

Dealership, G. Marshall & Sons with branches in Amersham and Chesham. The new company continued to develop. In 1992 new premises were bought in Staveley from Autoworld and in 1993 new premises in Somercotes, Alfreton were acquired from Kettles. Also the Amersham territory was extended to High Wycombe and a large dealership was developed on London Road.

Ford's new sales territory plans have resulted in the sale of Sheffield and High Wycombe and GK Group are now concentrating on substantial expansion in the Midlands in the next few years.

Above: A Ford Zodiac on display in the 1960s.
Top: George Kenning Ford Dealership in Vicar Lane, Chesterfield. The business moved to its present premises in Chatsworth Road in 1966.
Left: A view of GK Group's site at Chatsworth Road, undergoing redevelopment in 1998.

'Tis not the walls that make the school

Mount St. Mary's College in its present form was opened on 17th September 1842, although there has been a scholastic presence on the site since the mid 1600s. The opening of the college was the brain-child of just one man, Fr. Randal Lythgoe. His original intentions were to provide a "liberal course of education on a plan sufficiently economical to place it within the reach of persons with large families and of small fortunes".

Intentions were modest. Spinkhill College, as it was known in the first year of its life, could cater for just thirty pupils but the instant popularity of the school meant that before long it was groaning under the weight of new intakes. By 1865, the superior anticipated 120 new arrivals, despite the fact that the College could cater for just a quarter of that. And the problem didn't get any better; a report from 1873 stated that 'We simply squeezed in and the College bulged outwards from the pressure.'

Numerous answers to the problem were adopted. Classes were abandoned for the under twelves, prospective boarders being turned away by the dozen. Further counter measures were the addition

Above: The old College taken in 1882.
Left: Our Lady of the Mount. This statue was erected in the 1880s.
Below: Shown in a 1939 prospectus for the College, this picture shows the Physical Training class, demonstrated by a group of sixth form pupils in the gymnasium.

the curriculum and social strata. One thing that has never altered however, is the dedication to Our Lady Immaculate. For a school rich in nostalgia and religious association, it is only fitting to note that the Mount once provided England with three fifths of her priests.

Now, although the curriculum has widened to include all of today's necessary instruction and the outlook is broader, the Mount has developed some of the more outward signs associated with other established schools; a more elaborate uniform, badges,

of wings to the original red stone building, Middleton Hall, and over the following years more adaptations (finances permitting) prevented the 'great squeeze' happening again.

Against this background of change, the curriculum also evolved. What was defined in 1843 as the 'Three R's' (reading, writing and arithmetic) grew to include geography, history, languages, algebra and trigonometry, the last two to be taught 'as required'.

Inevitably, over the last century and a half, the Mount has witnessed many changes in the pupils,

crests and colours. However, the simplistic ideals of its founder, Fr. Randal Lythgoe of providing a 'family unit as a home away from home' still hold firm today and commitment to the pupils within the walls is as strong as ever.

*Top: An aerial view of Mount St. Mary's College taken in the late 1930s. Above: A 1992 photograph of the old College from a different angle to the one on the opposite page. **Left:** Rhetoric House, pictured in a prospectus from 1996/7.*

Lifelong learning for the students of Chesterfield

Manor College stands on the site of the old Central School. Its foundation stones were laid on April 18th 1900 by Miss Violet Markham, a member of the Chesterfield gentry of the day, and Dr George Booth who was Chairman of the School Board.

The opening
The finished building was opened the following year by His Grace, the Duke of Devonshire and work commenced on June 3rd.

The school stood on a steep slope. Although this made for dangerous playgrounds, the advantage was the possibility of building a swimming bath in the basement.

It was a large one, fitted with diving boards, changing accommodation and seats for spectators and was the first bath to be attached to an elementary school in the whole country.

The school accommodated 1,202 children, more than the Board had in all its schools put together for the first 13 years of the new Central School's existence.

New additions
Plans were made in the late 20s to make it suitable for just senior boys and girls. Electric light installation, the provision of staffrooms and a boys' science room were deemed necessary and proposals for this work were submitted to the Board in February 1930 at an estimated cost of approximately £1,700.

> **"OVER 1000 STUDENTS ENROLLED IN THE FIRST WEEK OF OPENING AS AN F.E. CENTRE IN APRIL 1997."**

When the actual cost exceeded the estimate by £163. The deficit was made up by a loan from the Board of Education and the Ministry of Health. The bill for furnishings came to just £581 19s 11d.

Soon afterwards two improvements were added. The boys were provided with gymnasium equipment and the girls with a stage in the hall, two thirds of the cost of which the girls raised themselves. The girls were taught no science, though the authorities did admit that this was a deficiency.

An asset to the town
It was a school with a community focus, its pool not only for school use but a welcome asset to the town. A 'Settlement Class' for children who were mentally or physically handicapped, ('defective' was the contemporary term,) was loosely attached to the Central School.

Mr F A Croft, headmaster of the school in the 1940s collaborated with Mr A Greenough to write a book about the work in a 'New Secondary Modern School' after the 1944 Education act.

His aims for education still apply today. "...to consider the community of which the child is a member, to help to discover the educational needs in relation to this community; to assess accurately aptitudes and abilities and devise a curriculum designed to promote maximum educational development." When further government reorganisation brought comprehensive schools into being, Manor developed into a two-site community school which ran successfully until the early nineties. Then, under tertiary reorganisation the site closed as a school.

New beginnings
In November 1995, North Derbyshire Tertiary, a Further Education Corporation, bought the building from the local authority and named it Manor College FE Centre. It opened as a community college after considerable renovation and refurbishment. It was the first college in the area to be open seven days a week, fifty weeks of the year. Its courses are varied, ranging from Aromatherapy to Information Technology. Working on the sensible premise that it does no good to lecture on abstruse subjects to a handful of students the college follows the demand, providing courses that meet the needs of the community and employers.

The aim of its staff and management is 'Lifelong Learning in a welcoming environment to the community and workforce of Chesterfield and surrounding locations'.

Above: The modern interior of the school.
Facing page: The beautiful building lit up at night.

Coalite - what's in a name?

Coalite was the brainwave of an eminent Victorian engineer called Thomas Parker who patented the Low Temperature Carbonisation Process in 1906 (half a century before the Clean Air Act was introduced by Parliament). To say he was a man ahead of time is an understatement.

A sample of Coalite was submitted to the City, to raise finances for his venture. As a result of this, British Coalite Ltd was formed.

Unfortunately, Thomas Parker never lived long enough to see his idea in full scale production. Sadly he died in 1915, two years before the company that was to become the forerunner of Coalite Smokeless Fuels was established.

Production of Coalite began at Barugh near Barnsley. By the late 1920s two further plants were opened at Askern near Doncaster and at East

Greenwich in London. The latter was operated under licence by the South Metropolitan Gas Company.

Demand for Coalite increased and by 1932 over 225,000 tonnes of Coalite were being produced annually. This was in addition to 26,000 barrels of crude oil; 1,290 million cubic feet of gas and 800,000 gallons of petrol.

It is a little known fact that raw materials extracted from coal to make Coalite can be used to produce crude oil and petrol. In the 1930s, at the height of the Great

Above and left: Delivery of Coalite during the 1930s. The transportation methods altered drastically in the 30s. Horse power was gradually phased out as the decade came to an end and motorisation, which was quicker and more efficient meant that the company's products became available to a much larger customer base.

Depression and with the Second World War looming, these proved to be vital to Britain's economy, fuelling 20 squadrons of the RAF and a number of Royal Navy ships.

Nowadays, the by-products of the Coalite process are refined into chemicals for a variety of industries. During the 1930s the company continued to grow. In 1933 Coalite became the first company to introduce pre-pack bags with a 14lb carrier bag for flat dwellers and people with limited storage space.

Four years later, on 14 April 1937, the company's present works at Bolsover were officially opened by the Duke of Kent. At the time it was described as "the largest plant of its kind in the world". In 1939 production was further enhanced with the addition on another works in Wern Tarn, South Wales.

meant towns and cities were often blanketed by a permanent smog. In the 1950s this led to ten city councils, led by Coventry and Manchester, establishing 'smokeless zones'.

However, it wasn't until the devastating London smog of 1952 when 4,000 people died that the government of the day took action and introduced the Clean Air Act.

This gave the company extra impetus, and even had city councils asking Coalite to increase production as areas were declared smokeless zones.

Older plants were closed as Bolsover and Askern were expanded. A year before the company's

Households were demanding smokeless coal and Coalite. It's important to remember at the time natural gas was unheard of. By and large, the country was kept warm by and, in a lot of instances, cooked using coal.

On still winter days this

Above: A 1955 advertising campaign, showing a young girl in a warm orange dressing gown standing before a Coalite fire.
Top: Barugh Works in 1927.
Right: Two 1940s delivery vans.

Golden Jubilee in 1966 a new works was opened at Grimethorpe near Barnsley.

During the 1970s and 1980s the Coalite Group continued to expand. With the advent of natural gas and subsequent decline in the UK market for all types of solid fuel, Coalite moved into other markets.

Businesses included builders merchants, car distributors, fuel and oil distributors, specialist vehicle manufacturers, transport and warehousing companies, docks and shipping interests, oil production and exploration and substantial interests in the Falkland Islands.

Above: The Duke of Kent at the official opening of the Bolsover Works in 1937.
Right: A 1950s carnival float with the Coalite Cats in silhouette in the background.

Today, production has been concentrated at the company's Bolsover plant. Three types of fuels are produced to suit most types of solid fuel appliances.

Thomas Parker's process is still used today to make Coalite. Only specially selected grades of

British mined coal are used. They are blended and undergo a process known as Low Temperature Carbonisation to leave a premium quality smokeless coal.

Technology may have intervened in the subsequent years, but the process remains fundamentally the same. In an ever changing world, it is heartening to know that since Thomas Parker first patented a smokeless coal, Coalite has remained true to his original idea.

Like Heinz and baked beans or Kellogg's and corn flakes, Coalite is synonymous with smokeless coal and real fires. It's Britain's favourite - more people choose Coalite than any other type of smokeless coal. For the open fire, there's traditional Coalite or Coalite Large as it is often referred to. Alternatively, for roomheaters, most boilers and cookers, there's Coalite Nuts - a smaller sized version of normal Coalite and for today's modern roomheaters, Coalite Blazebrite.

They're qualities that established Coalite as Britain's favourite

smokeless coal and will no doubt be enjoyed by millions of people with real fires well into the next millennium.

Above: The Coalite Cats became as famous as the product they advertised.
Top: Another carnival float from the 1970s.
Left: The Coalite Shire Horse Team.

Frederick's Ice Cream - the flavour of the Peak

The origins of Frederick's Ice Cream can be traced back to Parma, Northern Italy in the late 1800s. The present partner's grandfather and founder great-grandfather Angelo came to England from Italy around 1870 and started his own ice cream business in the Paradise Street/Meadow Lane area in Sheffield in the late 1890s after arriving from his home town in Italy.

The company's links with Chesterfield go back over seventy years to 1925. Angelo's son John, who traded as John Russell, followed in the family footsteps and moved his business to Chesterfield from Sheffield in 1925, starting from the Star & Garter Yard, Lowerpavement then moving to Old Hall Road, setting up at Number 88 in August 1947.

John Russell's daughter Pauline later married Bruno Frederick, whose grandfather was in the ice cream industry in Atherton in the 1900s. Bruno carried on the tradition and the company eventually became known as Frederick's in the 1950s.

Bruno and Pauline are now Senior Executive partners in the company which includes their son and two daughters.

John Frederick is Managing Director of the business with Louisa Taaffe the Events Executive and Head of Personnel and Julie Frederick heading the sales division.

During the early years the family developed their own recipe for Italian ice cream which was brought over in the 1870s. The traditional brands of Vanilla and Dairy ices, using the finest ingredients are still being produced to this day.

The company became a member of the National Ice Cream Alliance in 1956. The prime objective of joining the N.I.C.A. was to establish Frederick's Traditional Ice Cream on the national register putting it in direct contact via competitions with the best ice cream makers in the British Isles.

The company has participated in the N.I.C.A. competitions continuously since joining in 1956 and has won numerous awards every year ranging from the prestigious "Silver Challenge Cup" which it has won 3 times the highest award achievable, 2 Silver and 2 Bronze Medals, Special Diploma of Merits and Diplomas of various ranks.

Above: John Russell pictured in the 1930s outside the Star & Garter Yard premises, where the company's connection with Chesterfield began.
Left: Bruno Frederick can be seen on the far right of this charming 1950s photograph.

The company has won over seventy awards throughout the years, nearly as many as they have been in business in Chesterfield. They intend to win many more to maintain their title of "Award Winning Ice Cream".

The business has moved away from its original way of selling, which was mobile street hawking, to a more structured and permanent operation of retailing. This is now carried out from vans and kiosks situated throughout Chesterfield and the Peak District on licensed sites. These are owned or managed by the local Council, Peak National Park, National Trust and English Heritage. The company also supplies the Angling Fair (Chatsworth), the Bakewell Show, the Ashover Show and the Chatsworth Country Fair.

The company is shaping up to meet the demands of the Millennium by updating their mobile operation using the latest Ford Transit Vans coach built by Whitby Engineering furnished with the best technical equipment which helps maintain the quality of their ice cream and incorporated with the latest hygienic and up-to-date facilities.

Above: A trailer in the Market Square in the mid 1960s.
Left: A Morris Commercial PV van from 1953. This vehicle has been restored recently by the company.

The company has close associations with the National Trust and Hardwick Hall. Frederick's were asked to produce an "Elizabethan Ice Cream" for the 400th Anniversary of Hardwick Hall.

Below: The Frederick family from left to right; Pauline Frederick, Julie Frederick, Bruno Frederick and Louise Taaffe.

The company also produced a blue and white ice cream called the "Spirite Special" which was made to honour Chesterfield Football Club's great achievement in reaching the semi-finals of the F.A. Cup in April 1997.

Frederick's of Chesterfield will be celebrating their Centenary this year (1998) as well as selling their traditional 1898 flavour they will also be producing a special "Centenary flavour'.

Brampton Bakery - The staff of life for Chesterfield

The original title of the firm that began business at 294A Chatsworth Road, Brampton, was Brampton Steam Bakery. This was because the bakehouse ovens were heated by super-heated steam. It was produced by coke firing which burnt in equipment which was made by Hunts of Leicester. The steam passed through tubes that led into the furnace at the back of the ovens.

The bread was removed from the ovens with wooden peels and the freshly-baked bread was delivered in a covered wagon pulled by horses. On the whole, business flourished with only minor problems. During the two wars there was a shortage of raw materials and government subsidies kept down the price of a loaf - to a penny during the first war.

Up to the forties public baking was done. People mixed bread dough at home and brought it along to have it baked in the bakehouse ovens. Since then the business has continued to work through two strikes by the nations bread bakers which earned it the respect of its customers.

The business was set up some time between 1895 and 1900 by John Clarke, the great grandfather of David Clarke, one of the three current partners. He was helped by his wife, Sarah Anne. Over the years, the business passed first

Above: A beautiful turn of the century photograph of the Clarke family with John Clarke on the left.
Left: Luther, John's son who took over the business after his father's death. He was the second generation of the Clarke family to run the firm.

to John's son, Luther Clarke, then to Luther's son, Alfred Reginald (Reg).

Now there have been four generations of Clarkes in the business. David Clarke worked in the bakehouse after he left school until 1973 when he went to Australia for three years. The bakery was run as a one-man business till 1977 when Reg retired. After that, his son David went into partnership with his lifelong friend, Michael Smith (Mick). Mick, as a schoolboy had earned pocket money by working at the bakery on Saturday mornings.

In the eighties the bakery moved its premises to the Warwick Park Industrial Estate at Storforth Lane and David Shaw also became a full partner.

Nowadays the bakery has modern electric ovens and delivers its bread and other products in a fleet of vans. They make rolls, crusty and soft bread, pizza bases, scones etc. and send them to customers throughout Yorkshire, Derbyshire, Nottinghamshire and Staffordshire.

The customers are cash and carry businesses, restaurants, supermarkets and pubs. The bakery is a century old and its staff, consisting currently of twenty people, intend to serve the public equally well for another hundred years.

> "UP TO THE 1940S PEOPLE MIXED DOUGH AT HOME AND TOOK IT TO THE BAKERY TO HAVE IT BAKED IN THE OVENS."

Above left: Alfred Reginald (Reg) Clarke, third generation of the family.
Below: Mick Smith in 1979, showing the traditional ovens used in the bakery.

Proud of its past - confident of its future

IN the year of 1875, during Queen Victoria's reign, Isaac Eyre was living and working in Barrow Hill. At that time, he had no idea of the part he and his descendants would play in the creation of one of the largest furniture stores in Great Britain.

It was only after an injury sustained at work, leaving him unable to continue in his line of employment, that it became necessary for him to find other means of a livelihood for his family. Social Security at that time depended on a man's fitness and willingness to work, and upon what he had saved for a 'rainy day'.

Isaac began by selling sewing machines and mangles, and his personality made him many friends amongst his customers. This meant that before long, his business (which had been conducted from his home) had to be moved into a shop within yards of Chesterfield's famous crooked spire. There, for the first time he was able to display his wares for passers-by to see. The company had become established.

Isaac and his son continued to develop the premises at the rear and went into furniture manufacture, employing nine cabinet makers, polishers and upholsterers.

The demand for the shop-made furniture increased to such an extent that Isaac was able to purchase new premises in Tapton Lane where they installed their first wood-working machinery, employing 37 people. Within fifteen years Isaac Eyre & Son had such a reputation that people came from miles around.

The First World War brought hardship to the company, as it did with most. Many of the company's newly acquired vehicles were requisitioned by the Government and many of its staff joined the forces. But, after the decrease in the demand for new furniture during the war years, peacetime brought them almost insatiable requests for their products.

World War II brought about similar problems, with two thirds of Eyres' premises being requisitioned by the Ministry of Supply for the storage of textiles. At that time, only essential work was permissible. Managing Director, Charles Summers, the great-great grandson of Isaac Eyres is proud of the fact that the company is still run by the same family today, over a century later.

The company has expanded the premises so much that it takes up the whole of the building and its customer base is country wide. The traditional approach initiated by Isaac Eyres has continued to run through the business, courtesy and quality service are instilled into the staff.

What began as an accident in 1875 has grown into one of the area's leading furniture companies today and with a history as diverse and rich as it has had, the future is equally as bright.

*Above: Eyres' 1940s fleet of delivery trucks which during 1949 delivered furnishings to over 100 homes per day. **Top left:** Isaac Eyre, founder of the company. **Top:** Eyres of Chesterfield as seen in the late 1940s. **Left:** A traction engine that was used for big removals at the turn of the century. This one was decorated to take part in a local procession.*

Sympathetic, professional and helpful service to the local community

The origin of Crowder & Alderson Funeral Services was a business set up late in the 19th century by a Mr Henry Alderson. He had been a builder and called his new concern Alderson Funeral Service.

His business passed to a relative, Jack Alderson who was the last of the owners to bear the family name. Jack spent all his working life with the firm and died in 1963. His widow carried on the business which at that time was situated in St John's Road, Newbold. She received help from another funeral director, Graham Crowder whose business was on Avenue Road.

When Mrs Alderson retired in the seventies she sold her business to Graham Crowder who

> **"QUALITY IN FOCUS IS A MOTTO ADOPTED BY THE COMPANY AND IS A GUARANTEE OF THE SERVICE OFFERED."**

The firm's motto is 'Quality in Focus', which is Crowder and Alderson's guarantee of a good, sympathetic, professional and helpful service at a time, for the client, of great vulnerability and need.

The business hopes to continue to serve the community, particularly in Old Whittington, for many years.

Left: A vehicle from the current fleet.
Below: Pat Willerton and Margaret Tickner, the funeral directors.

incorporated both names into the title and moved to Whitting Valley Road, Old Whittington where the business still continues today. Thus, Crowder and Alderson came into being.

After Graham Crowder's death in 1980 the firm changed hands several times, so that it was no longer an independent, family-run affair. Nevertheless, the personal attention to each client, which is essential in this profession, is still the most important element to the present manager, Ethel McMurdo, and the two lady funeral directors, Pat Willerton and Margaret Tickner.

Modern thinking and traditional values lead to success for Bothams

W.D. Botham & Sons (known as Bothams) was founded in 1871 by William Drabble Botham, the great Grandfather of the present partner, Mr William Derek Botham. A local butcher of repute, well known in the local farming community, William Drabble Botham took out an Auctioneers Licence on 11th July 1872, holding his first auction sale outside the Angel Hotel, Chesterfield later that month.

Originally trading from Chesterfield's historic Market Hall, William's second son, Joseph Archdale Botham was taken into partnership around 1890. In turn, Joseph's two sons William Colledge and Joseph Archdale Junior were taken into partnership circa 1925. The firm traded under the name of W.D. Botham & Sons, subsequently moving to larger, more suitable premises at Low Pavement.

William Colledge Botham qualified as an Agricultural Auctioneer, specialising in agricultural sales and valuations, playing a major role in the development of Chesterfield Cattle Market with

> "WD BOTHAM TOOK OUT AN AUCTIONEERS LICENCE ON 11TH JULY 1872 AND HELD HIS FIRST SALE LATER THAT SAME MONTH."

which the firm remained closely connected until the market closed in the 1970s.

Following the untimely death of Joseph Archdale Botham, William Colledge continued in sole practice throughout the Second World War until he took his two sons, William Derek and John Knighton into partnership in 1958. At that time he also took on another partner, John Edward Shemwell.

Whilst the practice continued professional agricultural work, in the post war period it had to diversify in response to the changing and developing property market of the 1960s. Derek Botham and Jack Shemwell specialised in agricultural and other professional valuation work, whilst John Botham developed the residential property sales side of the business into one of the area's leading and longest established Independent Estate Agency firms, with a fine reputation based upon family traditions, unrivalled experience and integrity from those early beginnings in 1871.

In advance of Chesterfield's award winning redevelopment scheme of the late

JOSEPH LEE, deceased.

Particulars of Sale and Plan

OF

Freehold Shop, House, Bakehouse and Premises, and Nine Cottages,

IN

HIGH STREET, CHESTERFIELD,

TO BE OFFERED FOR SALE BY

MESSRS.

W. D. BOTHAM & SONS

AT THE

"ANGEL" HOTEL, CHESTERFIELD,

ON

THURSDAY, 27th October, 1910,

at 6-30 p.m. prompt.

H. E. WARD & Co.,
SOLICITORS,
CHESTERFIELD.

1970s, the firm relocated to purpose built premises at West Bars House in 1975, where it has remained ever since. This prominent town centre sales office provides an excellent base for successfully marketing a wide range of property in Chesterfield and North Derbyshire, together with a full range of professional property valuation services.

As an example of the wide range of properties available Bothams sold the first private residential property in Chesterfield to realise in excess of £100,000 circa 1982. Fifteen years later, residential sales have ranged from as low as £10,000 to a negotiated sale in excess of £1,000,000.

During 1982, Alan James Terry was taken into partnership, initially assisting John Botham with increasing residential sales and valuation work, subsequently expanding the firm's professional valuation activities and developing the commercial and industrial property section which now forms a significant part of the firm's business.

Prior to the more recent retirements of Jack Shemwell and John Botham, Derek Botham and Alan Terry were joined in partnership by Peter Bagnall and Mike Hinch, all born and bred in Chesterfield, locally experienced Chartered Surveyors able to offer unrivalled professional experience and knowledge, continuing the established theme of this family partnership which has continually developed to meet new challenges and change since 1871 to the present time.

To help the firm move with the times, it installed computerised systems in the mid 1980s, with a particularly effective wide ranging property mailing list system. The technology has been updated since that time, further developing their position as one of the town's leading, long established, independent Estate Agents, Chartered Surveyors and Valuers.

During its long history since that first auction in 1872, the firm was an early pioneer in the use of photography for property marketing purposes. The colour photographs incorporated within most

agency particulars were introduced to Chesterfield by Bothams.

Commercial and private sales include a wide range of residential, commercial and industrial properties. The firm also offers a professional valuation service to lenders including most banks and building societies.

Proud of its reputation over the last 127 years of service in Chesterfield and North Derbyshire, the firm's present partnership continues to keenly uphold traditional values, offering unrivalled local knowledge and total independence on business matters. Modern thinking, helpful service and the traditional values lead to successful sales, with every client's needs being of paramount importance. It is these values that have allowed the firm to grow and it is these values that will lead it firmly into the next century.

Right: The five partners of Bothams. Standing (left to right); M. T. Hinch, P. Bagnall. and A.J. Terry. Sitting; J.K. Botham and W.D. Botham. Since this picture was taken John Botham (sitting on the left) has retired.

Above left: An auction held in October 1910.

Facing page, top left: W.D. Botham, a local butcher who changed careers to become the founder of the oldest independent Estate Agency in Chesterfield.

Facing page, bottom: Bothams worked with another auctioneer to run the Chesterfield Fat Stock Show in the 1930s.

Below: The modern premises in West Bars House.

ACKNOWLEDGMENTS

THANKS ARE DUE TO THE FOLLOWING PEOPLE
AND ORGANISATIONS FOR HELPING TO MAKE
THIS BOOK POSSIBLE:

MR. G.W. MARTIN

DERBYSHIRE COUNTY COUNCIL LIBRARIES
AND HERITAGE DEPARTMENT

MR. J. LILLEY, LOCAL STUDIES LIBRARIAN
CHESTERFIELD LIBRARY

THE LATE MR. R. WILSHER, A.R.P.S

MR. J. HARDY

MR. H. TURNER

MRS. V. YOUNG

MISS J. BOND